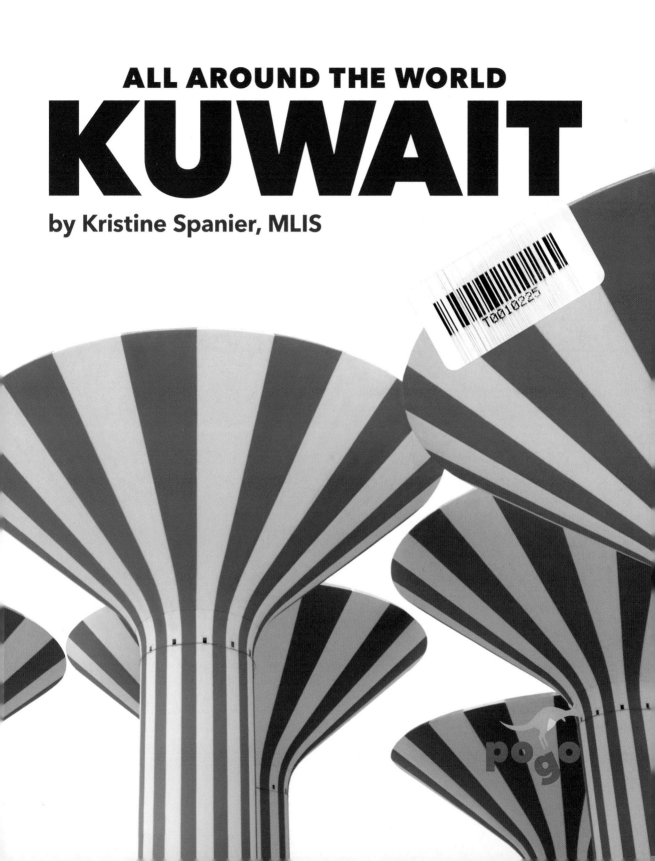

ALL AROUND THE WORLD
KUWAIT

by Kristine Spanier, MLIS

pogo

Ideas for Parents and Teachers

Pogo Books let children practice reading informational text while introducing them to nonfiction features such as headings, labels, sidebars, maps, and diagrams, as well as a table of contents, glossary, and index.

Carefully leveled text with a strong photo match offers early fluent readers the support they need to succeed.

Before Reading

- "Walk" through the book and point out the various nonfiction features. Ask the student what purpose each feature serves.
- Look at the glossary together. Read and discuss the words.

Read the Book

- Have the child read the book independently.
- Invite him or her to list questions that arise from reading.

After Reading

- Discuss the child's questions. Talk about how he or she might find answers to those questions.
- Prompt the child to think more. Ask: What did you know about Kuwait before you read this book? What more would you like to learn?

Pogo Books are published by Jump!
5357 Penn Avenue South
Minneapolis, MN 55419
www.jumplibrary.com

Library of Congress Cataloging-in-Publication Data

Names: Spanier, Kristine, author.
Title: Kuwait / Kristine Spanier.
Description: Minneapolis, MN: Jump!, Inc., 2022.
Series: All around the world
Includes index. | Audience: Ages 7-10
Identifiers: LCCN 2020054247 (print)
LCCN 2020054248 (ebook)
ISBN 9781636900087 (hardcover)
ISBN 9781636900094 (paperback)
ISBN 9781636900100 (ebook)
Subjects: LCSH: Kuwait—Juvenile literature.
Kuwait—Social life and customs—Juvenile literature.
Classification: LCC DS247.K8 S73 2022 (print)
LCC DS247.K8 (ebook) | DDC 953.67—dc23
LC record available at https://lccn.loc.gov/2020054247
LC ebook record available at https://lccn.loc.gov/2020054248

Editor: Jenna Gleisner
Designer: Molly Ballanger

Photo Credits: Faraj B/Shutterstock, cover; Lingbeek/iStock, 1; Pixfiction/Shutterstock, 3; Typhoonski/Dreamstime, 4, 10; Lukas Bischoff Photograph/Shutterstock, 5; Benkrut/Dreamstime, 6-7; Konrad Wothe/Minden Pictures/SuperStock, 8-9tl; Kertu/Shutterstock, 8-9tr; Nature Picture Library/Alamy, 8-9bl; Michael & Patricia Fogden/Minden Pictures/SuperStock, 8-9br; AP Images, 11; Michael Runkel/robertharding/SuperStock, 12-13; Danita Delimont/Alamy, 14-15; Kravtzov/Shutterstock, 16tl; HandmadePictures/Shutterstock, 16tr; Sinung Wahyono/Shutterstock, 16b; trabantos/Shutterstock, 17; Leonid Andronov/iStock, 18-19; REUTERS/Alamy, 20-21; Janusz Pienkowski/Shutterstock, 23.

Printed in the United States of America at Corporate Graphics in North Mankato, Minnesota.

TABLE OF CONTENTS

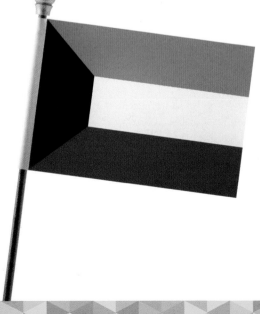

CHAPTER 1

IN THE DESERT

Welcome to Kuwait! Here, you can visit the Kuwait Towers. Inside, you will find a restaurant and a viewing **platform**.

platform

The platform is 404 feet (123 meters) high. It spins. People can look out over Kuwait City. This is the country's **capital**. It borders the Persian Gulf.

Persian Gulf

Kuwait is in the Middle East. The Arabian Desert covers most of the country. It is hot and dry here. Temperatures can be higher than 110 degrees Fahrenheit (43 degrees Celsius). It usually rains less than seven inches (18 centimeters) a year.

DID YOU KNOW?

Most of the water in Kuwait comes from the Arabian Sea. Salt must be removed for drinking. It is stored in water towers.

Animals here are suited to live in the desert. You may see a fennec fox or gazelle. The dab lizard also makes its home here. Look out for the Sahara sand viper! It has **venom**.

fennec fox

gazelle

dab lizard

Sahara sand viper

CHAPTER 2
LIFE IN KUWAIT

watchtower

This is the Seif Palace. Government leaders have met here since 1880. The watchtower has blue tiles. The roof is plated in real gold.

emir of Kuwait

Kuwait is an **emirate**. The Al-Sabah **Dynasty** has ruled since 1756. The **emir** is chosen from this family.

Grand Mosque

Most people here are **Muslim**. They **worship** in **mosques**. The Grand Mosque is the largest in Kuwait. It took seven years to build. There is room for more than 10,000 people inside!

Children begin school when they are six years old. They attend until they are 14. The government pays for school meals, books, and uniforms. **Transportation** to school is free, too.

WHAT DO YOU THINK?

After schooling, people may get jobs in the oil industry. Oil is a **natural resource** here. What jobs do people have where you live?

OIL

CHAPTER 3

FOOD AND FUN

Would you like to try fūl? This is fava beans with garlic and lemon. Falafel is fried balls of spiced chickpeas. Khubz is a flatbread. Spiced rice makes a complete meal.

fūl

falafel

khubz

Being so close to the gulf means water sports are popular. People jet ski, water ski, and windsurf. Some scuba dive. Others fish or sail.

Al Shaheed
Park

Al Shaheed Park is in Kuwait City. People gather here. They enjoy picnics. Some ride bikes on trails.

WHAT DO YOU THINK?

Kuwait is one of the most **urban** countries in the world. Almost everyone here lives in Kuwait City. Where do most people live in your state or country?

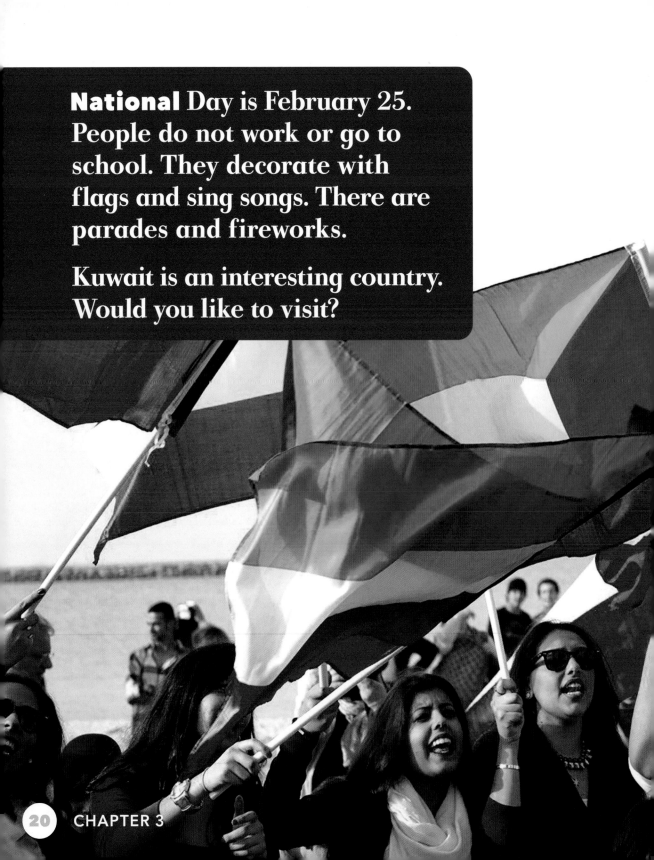

National Day is February 25. People do not work or go to school. They decorate with flags and sing songs. There are parades and fireworks.

Kuwait is an interesting country. Would you like to visit?

TAKE A LOOK!

The flag of Kuwait is important to its people.
What do its colors stand for? Take a look!

■ = rich fields
☐ = **purity**
■ = soldiers
■ = defeat of the enemy

QUICK FACTS & TOOLS

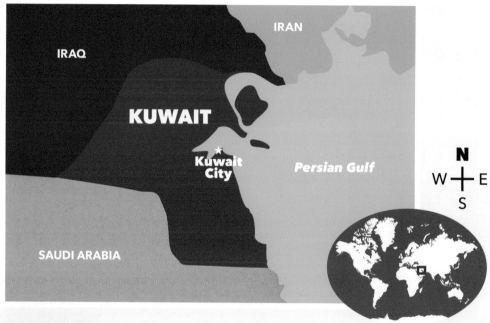

KUWAIT

Location: Middle East

Size: 6,880 square miles (17,819 square kilometers)

Population: 4,270,571 (July 2020 estimate)

Capital: Kuwait City

Type of Government: emirate

Languages: Arabic, English

Exports: oil and refined products, fertilizers

Currency: Kuwaiti dinar

GLOSSARY

capital: A city where government leaders meet.

dynasty: A series of rulers belonging to the same family.

emir: A ruler, chief, or commander in an Islamic country.

emirate: The state or country of an emir, or Islamic ruler.

mosques: Buildings where Muslims worship.

Muslim: A person whose religion is Islam.

national: Of, having to do with, or shared by a whole nation.

natural resource: A material produced by Earth that is necessary or useful to people.

platform: A flat, raised structure where people or objects can stand.

purity: The quality of being pure.

transportation: A means or system for moving people or things from one place to another.

urban: Having to do with or living in a city.

venom: Poison produced by some snakes and spiders.

worship: To show love and devotion to God or a god, especially by praying or going to a religious service.

Kuwait's currency

INDEX

TO LEARN MORE

Finding more information is as easy as 1, 2, 3.

❶ Go to www.factsurfer.com

❷ Enter "Kuwait" into the search box.

❸ Choose your book to see a list of websites.

FACT SURFER